Polycene

Polycene

Poetry of Our Age

RUSSELL E. WILLIS

RESOURCE *Publications* • Eugene, Oregon

POLYCENE
Poetry of Our Age

Resource Publications
An Imprint of Wipf and Stock Publishers
199 W. 8th Ave., Suite 3
Eugene, OR 97401

www.wipfandstock.com

PAPERBACK ISBN: 979-8-3852-8563-1
HARDCOVER ISBN: 979-8-3852-8564-8
EBOOK ISBN: 979-8-3852-8565-5

VERSION NUMBER 052826

To my two Billies,
The one who brought me into her world,
and the one who will inherit the world I've been working on
ever since.

echoing the wind,
for those who listen
there is in a single fluttering note
warning,
blessing,
old woman's sigh,
baby's cry.

If this is a game, play it out;
for it matters, these words,
often more than we imagine,
certainly more than we know.

Contents

Listening to the Winds

These poems were not written with a book in mind.

They emerged slowly over several years among many other poems, often beginning with nothing more than a moment of attention: an image that lingered, a phrase that would not leave, a question that seemed easier to approach through sound and weight than through argument or analysis.

Poetry arrived late for me, almost as if another kind of hearing had become necessary. Until my early sixties, much of my life had been spent working within systems—first as an engineer, then as a student and teacher exploring the complex institutions that shape human life, and ultimately as an entrepreneur applying technical advances across several human domains.

That work sought to understand how technological systems, social institutions, and moral choices interact in modern societies. It operated, necessarily, at the level of language: argument, analysis, the careful assignment of meaning to things already made conscious.

What poetry reached was something prior to that.

My adult life unfolded across a series of moments that, at first, arrived as background: the Cold War, the rise of environmental awareness, Y2K, a technologically driven global economy, the climate crisis, COVID, and now AI. Each emerged first as white noise—present, but not yet pressing its claim on consciousness. And yet, through that background hum, familiar landscapes began to appear subtly altered. Weather carried unfamiliar signals. The language of work, identity, and belonging shifted beneath our feet. Even ordinary moments—birds scattering from a tree, smoke in a distant sky, drinking a cup of coffee—began to feel like signals breaking through from background into foreground, not yet understood but no longer ignorable.

That is what listening means in these poems.

Not the decoding of messages already formed, but something closer to what an accent does before the words arrive—the way a parent's voice reaches a child at a level prior to meaning, already carrying warning, comfort, urgency, care. The single fluttering note that holds, for those willing to hear it, more than any word has yet named. Only recently, as I returned to prose to explore responsibility in the age of AI, did I realize that the poet in me had not stepped aside, but rather, inside. As I struggled to understand what journalist Thomas L. Friedman has called the *Polycene*—an age shaped not by one overwhelming force but by many at once, each amplifying the others—I recognized that I had already been living inside it.

And listening.

These poems are not arguments.

They are acts of listening to our age from the inside—before we fully name it, before we can decide what the single fluttering note might mean.

Listening to these winds.

Acknowledgements

Grateful acknowledgment is made to the editors of the following publications in which these poems first appeared:

Cathexis Northwest: "A Word for that Sound" (October 2022)

The Metaworker Literary Magazine, "Undisturbed" (2020).

The POET: "Black Gold's Siren Call" (*Family* issue, 2022); "Where Once Lay a Sprawling Lake" (*Earth* issue, 2023)

Tiny Seed Literary Journal: "Snake Tree" (April 2021)

Valiant Scribe: "Venetian Masks" (2021); "Dance of the *Cafeteros*" (July 2022)

The Write Launch: "Windsong: Solo Flute" (Issue 66, October 2022); "Reservoir No More" and "Earth Cries and the Oceans Catch the Tears" (*Climate Crisis* issue, Winter 2024)

The Writers Club: "We Are the Both" (December 2023)

I. Listening

is there a word in English
for that sound?

Windsong: Solo Flute

The flutes of those
who live
with,
not just in,
nature,
mimic windsong.

Even accidental noise
blown by untrained lips
echoes the haunting, ethereal
whistle of wind
through limbs and grass, crops and structures.

Artist adds
nuance and voice.
echoing the wind,
for those who listen
there is in a single fluttering note
    warning,
    blessing,
    old woman's sigh,
    baby's cry.

In the melody of windsong or flute can live
    tone poems of
        babbling brooks,
        wind through eagle's wings,
        calls from
            gulls dodging breakers on the shores of
            vast oceans,
            owls tracking prey in deep forests,
            loons standing quiet vigil in the shal-
            lows of uncharted
                lakes,

songs remembered and repeated to the seventh generation
love songs
lessons in patience
prayers
dreams
epic poems of the rise and fall of civilizations
long before the old world
became the New World,
music that is of Nature and humanity all at once
feeding, ordering, enlightening the soul.

This escapes most of us
who listen neither to the flutes (or their players)
nor the wind.
All we hear. . .
moans
phantom's shrieks
shrill sirens of Nature
disturbing our sleep,
interrupting our hike,
scaring the children, or
prompting us to hunker down for safety,
unsettling our souls.

A Word for that Sound

"Flapping" won't suffice
for the sound of scores
of Grackles fleeing from
over there behind those trees to
somewhere else beyond the house
that blocks my view.
Fleeing what, I'll never know, but
accepting "flap" to evoke
that moment simply
will not do; leaving me to wonder
if there is a word in English
for that sound, knowing with
certitude that there are languages
that do, or at least did, for
such language is often dead to us
along with those who spoke of
such things with awe and reverence
in a world passed by
by those who have no time or
reason for such thoughts,
and, therefore, no such words.

Snake Tree

Oh-dark-thirty on a Texas morning
By the calendar
          a spring day
          after a pitiful winter
                    even by Texas standards

A spring day that felt like the winter should have
          that marrow-chill you only get in the South
                    we never dress for it
                    but love to complain about how cold it is
                    after spending most of the rest of our waking
          hours
                              complaining about how hot it is

There was actually ice on the
          edge of the lake in our little cove
          and on the branches of the newly-budding tree
          listing out over the water
Like many trees in Texas
          not much more than a scrawny shrub with a trunk
But just as I reached out to snap off a limb to make the ice crack

I stopped cold

(yeh, I know, pretty lame!)

On virtually every limb
          a small snake
          one to two rulers long

                    a cotton head -- water mocassin
                    a dangerous snake when not frozen to a limb
                    the tell-tale delta-shaped head
                    attached to a rigid length of cord
                    draped around a brittle limb
                    dangling out over the
                    partially frozen cove

Hatched not long ago during the faux spring
          following a faux winter
Caught by the freeze
          Hibernating in isolation, each on its own limb

At twelve-years-old
          I'd never seen a snake tree before
I never have since
(though I know now its called brumation, not hibernation)
Nevertheless. . .I wonder why I thought of that just now?

Clear Days

Brilliant blue sky
Canopy inlaid with sun
Crystal clarity
Separating earth from eternity
No rain or snow or mist or fog
Nor even wisps of cloud or
Radiant distortions
To disturb the view

This visual vacuum sucks
Soul out of body
Mind out of brain
Consciousness out of self
Gravity on holiday
Not soaring or floating
Which requires lift
But freedom
Spirit unencumbered
Not reactionary restlessness
But creative peace
To be life-giving and
Breathtaking in the same moment
Not sensed, yet
Excruciatingly real

For that moment
Clarity to be treasured

For the next moment is life
In relentless cycles of
Winter's fog and snow and creeping night, or
Summer's rain and windblown dust and endless days

Reservoir No More

seas rise as lakebeds crumble into dust

parched earth stares at heaven
with blank, bloodshot eyes

nothing moves unless blown
by heart-broken winds,
scattering dust, rendering no relief
as waves of heat mimic breath

nothing moves since nothing lives
where water has ceased to visit
having sought refuge in the sea
in the face of an unrelenting foe

White Noise of Being

If I wasn't listening so hard
I would hear the white noise of being

Breaths escaping unbidden as sighs
birds welcoming the sun
or bidding the dusk
rustlings of uncountable sorts
doors slamming shut
music clinging to the air
and the air, playing the instruments
of our culture's ensemble--
windchimes, curtains, flags,
the paper detritus of even this
virtual sort of living

But all of that drowned
by the screaming silence of
you not coming up the drive
or through that door

II. The Planet Responds

the earth sighs

Earth Unaware

I hope the earth is unaware
of the inheritance we have squandered
and the delight that we have robbed.

But, there are sighs disguised as wind,
tears that fall as floods,
quaking fears tearing at seams,
boiling anger wildly flaring.

If only we would sigh and cry
and fear what we have wrought,
and loath that we can't stop.

The Earth Still Has Its Say

Though at night
From high above
The artificial reigns,
The contours of the light –
The graceful sway
Of river seams in culture's quilt,
The sharpness of the coastal edge
That cuts through human hubris –
Those lights below remind us yet
That earth still has its say

From Above at Night

From above at night
It all looks so warmly human

So bright and crisp the light
In the midst of deep darkness

So bright and beautiful its effect,
So many lights, so many souls

Some brilliantly packed.
Others sprinkled across the black

Vexing my mind and
Breaking my heart

Wondering if this is but a mirage
Or a sign of hope

Ashen Sky

A tepid sun turned falsely gold
A cloudless sky now ashen grey

What should have been a morning fog
A soup of poisoned promises

Of what might be of every dawn
As day's transfigured into night

And night into a sleepless fear
Of what we've done and failed to do

Of Floods and Ripping Tides

The water's grip comes as a surprise –
unsettling, strangling, overwhelming –
a monster's clutch as from another world
than surf or stream, arroyo or culvert.

Snatching out of time or place.
Fetching body and soul from one to another dimension;
black, cold, unrelenting, shifting, unfamiliar.
Pulled and pulled and pulled until a gasp, or purchase, or another's grip. . .

or nothing more . . .

. . . anymore

Undisturbed

Undisturbed, it gathers dust
until disturbed by accidental agency
sometimes disturbed by gentle strokes
so that it might appear, at least,
to be undisturbed by gathering dust,
or cleansed by drip or drop or flow or flood
or breeze or blow till left again undisturbed
only to gather dust again
some other dust, now with
similar consequence, similar enough
not to matter to the dust or what it strives to hide

The ocean floor comes to mind

a chessboard along the wall

shelves and the tops of books

ancient cities

memories

conscience

                                        and minds too long at rest, undisturbed
                              by thought,
                              and souls too long unmoved by empathy, or
          even sympathy,
          until to dust they return…
having remained too long undisturbed

Climate Changed

It's now a case of damage done.
Ground zero's in the past;
a relatively recent past
now passed to all our futures.

Our sin lies with our failure to repent,
to change, to plot a course from here,
the changed, to there, the might be less.

The more the less,
the more changed the changed,
the less the damage runs amok,
the less we face no more of this, of life.

The gift we must not squander;
for squandered it is already, and damaged.
And we the agents of demise must act.

humanature

How does this work? Are we
unique or simply part of a
manifold existence? Is intelligence
part of our nature or
yet another spiraling artifact? Do humans
answer only to other humans,
nodding occasionally to Transcendence? Or
are we in this
together, from top to bottom of life's
unrelenting complexity? Is there
room in human ego to accept that
everyone of us is part of it – Nature?

Where Once Lay a Sprawling Lake

All is stillness in the suffocating heat.
Vision dulls to a hazy glow, the air
Finding somewhere within the strength
To shimmer in the wake of this deep-space entropy.

Life dares not test the limits of fragility
At this edge of the goldilocks spectrum
Where salt and dust and skeletons of civilization
Bask where once lay a sprawling lake.

No longer the bed of the retreating expanse.
No longer even its beach, now only desert; the stage
Upon which the shimmer now dances its ballet of death
In the stillness of the suffocating heat.

At the Top and Bottom of the World

At the top and bottom of the world
As reckoned from the Equator
Both in and at the sea
And across mountain ranges
Hidden for eons by the whiteness
The whiteness surrenders

No matter that for all of recent centuries
Each cycle of the sun brought freeze and thaw
Unwitnessed by humans
An unrelenting battle for the sea
To be controlled by the domain of ice
Or to be freed to
Wash or rain or sweat as dew
To burst upon the shore or
Fall down rock faces into rivers
Ultimately feeding the seas
Along with cycles spanning years
With ages of ice or not
Cycles old and over long before history
Longer, much longer, than human memory
Unwitnessed, unconcerned

Even now, mostly witnessed by artificial eyes
Flying through the heavens on artificial moons
Now decoded by minds of our own devising
Relentlessly recording the relentless dance
Of ice and water
With instruments that notice that
This ice caused not by human guile but by nature
Captured the sea

The sea
Held hostage by the ice
Completely assimilated as ice

Yet still the sea
Its remnants decayed and squeezed
Melting frees the sea, not just as water
The Sea in all of its grandeur
Flora and fauna so foreign
To surface dwellers
The Sea released as water and methane
Methane, more potent than even
The gasses each human exhales and each tree inhales
In undoing or redoing climate

The unholy irony
The burning of fossil fuels from inside the Earth
Releases the gasses of fossil decay in eons-old ice
Adding insult to injury
Leveraging that which need be diminished
At the top and bottom of the world

Earth Cries and the Oceans Catch the Tears

Each corner of a globe
With no corners
Born of the sea as
Liquid or solid
In dances with humans
And dances between humans
Fear and hope meet in their own dance
As the earth cries
And the oceans catch the tears
And the tears are sensed
As warning signs
As storms measured in categories
As attitudes measured in politics
And the future measured in lives
And livelihoods

What category of ambition, idiocy or neglect
Will we deserve
If we ignore these categories?
What becomes of us who ignore the tears?
What becomes of us who forget the dance
Or refuse to dance
Or refuse to love the dancers?
Where lies our curiosity as we witness the tears?
What will trigger imagination in the face of our fears?
And what of the fears of others
When we think we have nothing to fear
And They come to fear Us?
And what of the evil unleashed
By self-inflicted ignorance
(not to mention arrogance)?

The Floods

Growing up in flood country
You know not to mess with floods
Don't cross a flooded street
Don't cross a flooded creek
Head to higher ground
Head to rocky ground
Don't be a fool
Head to higher ground
And don't ever begin to think
You are smarter or more powerful
Than a flood
Don't be a fool
You can't stop a flood
Head to higher ground
When the flood is coming
Stay calm
And head to higher ground

Be still
And know that I Am

III. Systems of Power

This spinning sphere has no top
or bottom — north and south, east or west,
except when we declare it so.

Black Gold's Siren Call

For all of his adult life
Dad followed a siren call
Along a trail of black gold
From bayous to the
Permian Basin and back
Sticking pins with colorful heads into
Maps with squiggly lines
Deciding where men with lots of money
Could drill wells that cost lots of money
In order to make lots more money, and so on

On the trail of black gold
The technology of sonar and radar
Developed during World War 2
Was connived to coax the remains of
Ancient seabeds and forests
And the creatures living therein
Into gas pumps on highways
And in small towns that
Witnessed the epic voyage
Of my Mom and Dad
And the other epic voyages of
Increasingly mobile Americans as they
Fled farms and that way of life
That had coaxed the teeming masses
From across the sea to embrace that way of life
        in my case, Scots-Irish and English
        Swiss-German and Dutch
        who through dislocation and relocation
        stumbled or jumped into
        marrying other strangers in this strange land
        even Irish brothers marrying Scottish sisters
        not to mention some of these immigrants
        marrying an American-American from time to time

They voyaged on ships powered ironically, but effectively,
by the original black gold, coal
which also came from the remains of
ancient sea beds and forests
and the creatures living therein
but was dug (not drilled)
by miners (not roughnecks)
(yet still controlled by men with lots of money
making even more money from miners, not
roughnecks)
for centuries before
geophysics degrees were granted
to young red-headed (and other-headed)
men (this was the '50s!) at Texas Tech
one of which was my Dad
But a new way of life was emerging
Built on a network of roadways
From suburban cul de sacs
To stretches of highway, like US 80
(one small section of which ran 440 miles
from near my parent's homes in Dallas
to my birthplace in Ft. Stockton)
That made mobile-America mobile
This new way of life being powered by
The newer version of black gold
That my Dad was chasing
In and around Texas

Dance of the *Cafeteros*

Far above the level of the sea
an Axis of Coffee straddles
the mountains of Colombia
For the *cafeteros* there is but
one centuries-old constant:
"there is always coffee"
But in this age
technology supplants
the marriage of
human and soil,
hands and limbs,
brains and beans.
The chase is on;
The chase to hold on
to the soil as it washes
off the mountains
The chase up the mountain,
ever higher,
chasing the temperatures
where coffee trees
thrive as lower altitudes
get warmer,
ever warmer.
This dance between
human and natural –
an ancient dance
The dance *cafeteros*
learned from their
abuelos y abuelas
The dance humans
had learned to do
with grace and finesse
and not a little bit of wisdom.

But not always;
sometimes heavy-handed
forgetting to dance.
Choosing, instead,
to simply use.
All the while,
the *cafeteros* push their hopes
and plantations
up the mountains
so that it may
still be true
in their world:
"there is always coffee"

Somewhere North of North Hampton

Cornrows roll past,
then a lake, a forest.
Civilization interspersed:
agriculture, small-town culture,
technologies spanning centuries,
then soybeans and solar panels --
acres of each in fields enclosed
with five kinds of fence.
Storm clouds roil westward --
can't see the sky to the east.
Serious weather to the west.

Smiles masked even as a
variant is mostly left behind,
yet clouding the future.
Empties streak by at
eighty miles per hour,
close enough to touch;
parked on sidings as if
arrayed on a shelf,
memories left behind --
the promises,
the dreams. . .

Whatever happened to those dreamers?
The trying to remember,
stuck now between past and future
when the view is blocked
by a huge solar panel array --
then slowing to stop at
Greenfield (how ironic!),
reminder of the promise,
or of the past,
or both, and
picking up speed as storm clouds build.

That Spinning Sphere

Hurtling through space
standing on a spinning sphere
we imagine the ground to be stationary

Watching the Sun and Moon rise and set
While the Sun hurtles through space
dragging Earth and Moon with it

Surrounded by millions of points of light
all hurtling through space themselves
each a sun or massive collection of suns

I had to learn that I am standing
on a spinning sphere hurtling
through space at an outrageous speed.

I learned this after many years
of having a globe around
Many globes, in fact, and pictures of globes

In school, libraries, museums
and that special one at home
with a light bulb inside

I have learned two things
From all of those globes
And some wise teachers on the side

To begin with, this spinning sphere has no top
or bottom -- north and south, east or west,
except when we declare it so by holding it a certain way

Some of the countries
printed on these globes have changed
War and politics and history have changed

Names have changed, boundaries
War and politics and peace - spins
On the surface of this spinning sphere

Humanity, grasping for life
as the sphere hurtles through space and
Time-what we call history

History, the story of standing on this
spinning sphere with others
Because this is our home

This sphere, hurtling as it is,
Is our home
This thing we share

When will the globe
(even the ones with light bulbs in them)
Become a symbol for home

Our home?
Our hope?
Ours?

Hidden Tornado

I still feel sad that I didn't get to see it.

They built the pool first in the middle of a scrub desert.
displays rendering the golf course to be. Late afternoon, though

because it was Summer, the sun was so high no one knew or
much cared that the day was retreating. Along the horizon,

the one to the West and a little bit north, it was growing, the thing,
it was growing; in pinkish-gray smoke it advanced and it grew
into "Storm!"

Once someone noticed, whether adult or child, in an instant it
Seemed the swimming was done. Kids plucked from the
water like lobsters before

a really fine meal, were guided to flip flops, wrapped up in
towels, tugged to the parking lot, thrown into cars and
ordered to get the windows up, NOW!

Sitting still wet in the car, caked in sand, wrapped in towels, the
adults set out through what was now a full gale. There was no
more sun and the

air was replaced with fine dust, hard to breathe, hard to see, as we
drove back to town past the old farmhouse we knew. Then the
rain fell in sheets

as the wind howled and tore. By that age I knew boats, and our
'54 Chevy had morphed into a foundering craft, inundated and
lost as the rain struck like

waves, then like bullets fired from the deck of the maurading vessel
through a darkness like night. But it was the noise that terrorized
most as my six-year-old

metaphors skipped through mind with each lightening flash
conjuring now the noise of a train. From some story I'd
heard, I conjured a train roaring

past on the road with no tracks to be seen. Utterly small our world
had become, the inside of a car in an ocean of storm with a
magnificent freight train flying beside.

Inside of a car, two moms and three boys were all of the universe,
all bathed in noise. Then suddenly, almost as fast as it left, the
world reappeared through the

windshield again. It was then that I learned about bats out of hell;
when my mother saw road the next stop would be home. It wasn't
until the next day

on the News that we learned a tornado had ravaged a house just
off the road to the new country club. They broadcast stock
footage: a two-story house that

had sat on that parcel for year upon year, until now. The eager
young man from the News showed a shot of a vacant slab
surrounded by shrubs and a tree stripped of

leaves, with a swing slowly swinging there still. "And that's all that
is left" at the spot near the road where two moms and three sons
through the storm had endured.

A half-century leapt, I am still amazed how often horizons
harbinger storms; how often we gather our loved ones around
to weather the tumult, retreat to our home;

how often some things we can't even see cause so much pain,
changing lives in a day. But I have to admit how empty I am

at not seeing the funnel strike down from the sky..

Categories (An Ode to Michael 10/10/2018)

Intellectual distinctions
Sets or subsets
Degrees of . . .

Making sense
Controlling attitude
Warning sign

Today, the mark of
Devastation of
Historical proportions

Crossing miles
Yet still 4
Cat's whisker away from 5

Deep in Georgia
Full effect
Though downgraded to 1

Born and bred in warmth
Warmth we've been warned about
Of our making!?

Making sense of
Those trying to control our attitudes
Toward warning signs

What category of ambition, idiocy or neglect
Will we deserve
If we ignore these categories?

Venice: Prosperity's Nightmares and Dreams

Following eons of becoming
A plain along a sea
Born of the Zanclean flood
And then centuries of
The march of ice
Across the adolescent continent marshland
A land composed mostly of water
A land of islands
A sanctuary difficult to tame
Even more difficult to invade
Became home to a people
Of pottery, then of copper, then of bronze
Of boats of bark to multi-masted ships of wood, then steel
Powered first by wind
Then steam from wood, then coal, then oil
Who knew uncertainty with certitude
Who lived on two edges
One constructed the other
What came to be of nature on
This fringe of the made
This come-to-be city in which the
Demarcation of city and canal
Civilization and Nature
Made and given
Continues to evolve
As masks hanging in shop windows
Drop imagined tears of sorrow and hope
From eyeholes above the painted frowns or smiles
Adding flow to the deluge of fear
Beholding prosperity's nightmares and dreams

Venetian Masks

Waters rise, drowning the square
St. Mark's afloat, a ship in danger of floundering
Its clock ringing out, a call of distress
And a mundane fact of life marking time
Grandeur muted by futility
Holiness sucked dry by fear as the square is inundated
The majestic lion, a cat not fond of a soggy swim

Around what was the teeming square
Tables and chairs are stacked inside
Robbed of conversation and laughter
Politics and romance
Floating fowl now rule
Where once doves skipped and swooped and
Stole scraps of baguettes and
Terrorized or delighted children by
Chasing or being chased

Behind the square
Demarcation of city and canal slowly dissolves
Masks hanging in shop windows
Display sorrow and hope in the painted frowns or smiles
The eye holes of the sorrowful drop imagined tears
Adding to the deluge of fear
The eyes of the hopeful behold St. Mark's and dream of
Canals agleam, doves above, awaiting permission to land

IV. Irish Need Not Apply

the sounds of home change

Joe, They Called Him

Joseph Russell
He was christened

His Barrett roots lie deep
In the soul of County Cork

His destiny lay across the pond,
Then half-way across a continent

Joe, they called him;
Leather, his trade

His shop throws shadows
From the cross's flames

His home fires bullied
By the cross's flames

Irish need not apply here
Irish need not live here

Joe, they called him,
Did not flinch

So immigrant blood
Flows through my veins

An immigrant's love
Lives through my name

Immigrant Blood Flows Through My Veins

Immigrant blood flows
Through the veins
Of those I know
And those I love,
Who are my us
But once were them
A mistrusted them
A hated them
An impure them
Until purified by common toil and
Common good and
Common sense
Until an us reveals
Until another them emerges
And common sense be damned
And common good
And common toil
'Till I am damned
Damned if I don't remember that
Immigrant blood flows
Through my veins

Accents

Embraced by accents familiar yet unaccustomed,
Familiar in the familiarity of the speakers

The knowing pauses, comfortable laughter,
Clucking tongues, sideways glances.

Discerning meaning without knowing the language,
Or better yet, feeling the meaning because

We feel for or with the speakers
Of these vaguely familiar words,

Accents speaking louder, clearer than words;
The different cradled by the familiar.

Comfortable and disaffected, for us to choose.
Embraced or put off, both powerfully emotive;

Gift and cost, gift or cost, at our discretion,
Not theirs (until, of course, they hear our accent).

When We Are *Us* and They Are *Them*

We are not our best
When we are *us* and they are *them*
When choosing who to love
Choose who needs to be loved
So that *us* expands and *other*
Dissolves into the mist of empathy
That we might be judged by the character of our heart
And not the blood that flows through it
By the home we open to others
Not the ground that lies beneath
By the comings together
Rather than the scatterings

Being-with

Being-with breaks the grammar of self
Selves-defined being
Mutual
Inter-dependent
Molecular ontology
The basis not of tribe
But of village, family
Of whatever "us" is
As distinguished from "Me,"
Not "them"

To want to be with,
A choice,
Is to want to be
In the fullest sense
A self

V. Living Inside Complexity

both are true

We Are the Both

We are the both
always competing
yet most of the time whole

When not our better self
too lazy is the good
too eager is the mean

Yet kind at random intervals
tears launched at pain
laughter loosed, tagging a passing joy

Sighs breathe in life, exhale fear
hands and lips touch
establishing We

Then in too many ways to count
so busy with Us
that We is set to simmer

Always in some measure
disdain in the driver's seat
kindness the back-seat driver

Despair shares a ride with hope
a dream in our pocket, fear in our gut
or is that vice-a-versa

Broken but not severed
wounded always
always healing

****

Until it comes that splinching
leaving us less, untreated, even then
a load no one should have to carry

Back, as if to birth
to find the lost
a new life promised

To pound at the door
for leave to enter
or to wake from the dead

Once found the work begins
labor for this new life
back, as if to birth

****

Better not to tempt
the one or either part to flee
better yet to keep the other's number close

To chat from time to time
hold tight to self
holding hands to safely cross the street

Exploring that which is new to both
Or common to the shared journey
To wish the better well and the other, Godspeed

Risk

Hope without risk
is mere expectation.
Life without risk
is mere existence.
So choose.
Choose to live in hope
or expect to merely exist.

Duplex

Tantalizingly simple complexity
thriving on similarity's eternal clash with entropy

Sitting there side by side
as if intimacy exacts no cost

As if relationship necessarily
begs the question of individualism

As if Yin and Yang weren't related
either by blood or by marriage

Two peas in a pod just before
the pea soup begins to simmer.

Black and White

I know what you're thinking.
It's never just black and white.

But why can't it be, just once –
as easy as black and white?

Even when it seems that simple,
Whatever it is is just part of all this.

These shades of gray!
God forbid if I start to feel blue!

Don't give me that look!
It's not my fault! Life happens!

The Thing Is

Black and white: the poles
not the thing itself

Black, the absence of the thing.
White, the thing undifferentiated.

I used to call the thing "gray,"
insisting that we clever ones

understood that the Real was
rendered in various shades of gray;

not black and white. No,
never that easy or cut and dry,

but messy, often dull, but
almost always messy. Gray.

Even the word for the thing
is messy: grey or gray?

And is a glass of grey liquid
half full or gray?

Then one day when I was old
I looked up and understood.

I knew I had been wrong.
I had always been wrong;

not totally wrong, but wrong enough
that it took my breath away.

Even after five degrees
and a nice piece of wallpaper

notifying all persons to whom
these presents shall come

that I am a certified expert of
thingness, I was wrong.

On that day I looked up
And everything had color.

Damn!
The thing was far more complicated

than I had dreamed, and I had
conjured substantial complexity,

even chaos, in my wakeful dreams.
The thing was more awful than

just messy, as in full of awe. I
wondered more at that which

could be wonderful (full of . . .) and
frightening and confusing at once.

Not only was the thing not simply
a battle between black and white,

it stretched from infinity
to the other side of infinity

with every color emerging from
another color, but only one other

color at a time in this timeless band
that never bent back over itself,

yet overlaid others as to
create and recreate their

infinite variety and common quality,
endless potential shades in every moment

cradling beauty else it carried
pain, joy, fear, comfort, exasperation,

desperation, elation, fear (yes,
a lot of fear) and more joy, and on

and on and on, this thing of beauty
and potential and all other values

in countless measures of good
and countless counter-measures of evil;

the whole thing in wobbly balance on the
point of something I can never really grasp

or measure other than to know that grasping and
measuring Good was somehow the point,

and that I should never be tempted
by gray (or even grey) again as the

best way to decide when right
and wrong is not good enough.

new normal -- a new path home

after sixty-six years
a first second-dose

another first in this
relentless year of nineteen

that has survived far too long
with fewer survivors

as the survivors long
for normal, but

create something else
or many something elses

that someday will
feel normal, even

tempting us along
new paths and away

from old temptations
that used to be the

temptations we relied on
to escape the norms;

even as now they may
be a new path home.

Hope Pushed into Time

Early hope is pulled by time
Carried on its wings
On the crest of its unfoldingness
Weightless in the scheme of things
Natural in its buoyancy and
Showing brightly in the light of days

Middle hope is braced by time
Carried still, but heavy now
Straining for attention
Among the shining things of life
Lived in the abundance of time
And times and time again

Later hope is pushed into time
Against the grain, against the tide
With fold-marks that tend to tear
Each time a wound or joy is opened
Many reopened through countless
Iterations of a day in the life

And yet across this span
Pulled by, braced by, pushed into time
Hope is hope
Light, shining, even creased
In its seasons
Always

VI. Progress?

What category of ambition, idiocy or neglect
will we deserve?

Quantum Mechanics of Hope

Each blank page is unique
A not yet, an infinite number of not-yets
Starting over in each moment as
Past expands and multiplies
Into futures not yet on this blank page
Which itself is unlike it was before the not yet
Poised to be filled
But unfulfilled in an emptiness that
Tempts the almost and
Paralyzes the what-if
And even when filled as 365 of 1000 copies
Its destiny is not that of 364 or 366
Even when it was just a blank page
A gift of indeterminable value and
Unfathomable potential
As unique and similar as any other
Though to be handled with care
Since hope needs be slippery
For if it's gripped too tight
We would never let go
And we'd surely be stuck
With a handful of ifs

Progress

In 1985 my first child was born.
I also wrote a paper about technology and responsibility (yes blogs used to be called "papers").
This was

nine years before there were any blogs,
fourteen years before the term "weblog" was coined,
five years before the human genome project officially began,
eighteen years before the human genome was fully mapped,
one year after Pakistan developed the means to produce a nuclear weapon,
twenty-one years before North Korea's first nuclear test,
nine years before the START treaty on nuclear nonproliferation began to be enforced,
four years *after the first* Space Shuttle flight,
twenty-six years *before the last* Space Shuttle flight,
ten years before the Hubble Telescope (which was launched by and later repaired on a Shuttle) took ten days to capture the Hubble Deep Field image containing 3,000 galaxies as they appeared 10 Billion years ago in a piece of the sky hiding behind a grain of rice held at arm's length,
ten years *after* the term "Global Warming" was coined to describe the worst-case scenario for climate, but
thirty years *before* the Paris Accords were signed (and thirty-two years *before* the United States withdrew from the Paris Accords),
ten years before the term "smartphone" was first used,
twelve years before the first hybrid car was mass-produced (The Toyota Prius),
twenty-nine years before Google revealed a prototype "autonomous" (driverless) car,

thirty seven years before generative AI entered a moment of genuine mass awareness

forty-one years before I published a book called *AI and the Crisis of Control*
(and 4 years before her brother, Ben was born).

During that same time of scientific and technological progress:
racism flourished,
sexism flourished,
war flourished,
greed flourished.
Now I look at the world that my generation and I are leaving to
Our now-grown children and their children and
I ask some questions:

Why, with all our science and technology,

we are smarter *and* less wise?
we are more eager to seek power than to be good?
we left our children's children (the generation of Columbine and Sandy Hook and Parkland and Santa Fe and Uvalde) the task of making us safe from the technology of death?

So even as I gaze again at the Deep Fields of Hubble and Webb,
and am awed by Creation,
I am sad for us.

Still,

It has only been forty-one years since Katherine was born, and
There appears to be more years for Katherine and Ben and their generation to make some progress.

Answering the Winds

These poems arise as attention does—unbidden, specific, impossible to predict. A sound beyond available English vocabulary. A landscape altered in ways that resist naming. The quiet awareness that familiar patterns may no longer hold.

The ordinary moments—a reservoir gone to dust, a place where there must always be coffee, a carnival mask crying tears for a disappearing civilization—carry signals larger than themselves.

The poems have done what poems can do.

Thomas L. Friedman gave this moment a name. The poems were already living inside it—an age shaped not only by the forces pressing upon it, but by how we respond to what we have heard.

This is the Polycene.

The answering is ours.

www.ingramcontent.com/pod-product-compliance
Lightning Source LLC
LaVergne TN
LVHW020657100826
845148LV00012B/2532